THE POETRY OF
NEIL MUNRO

WITH PREFACE BY
JOHN BUCHAN

SPA BOOKS

ISBN 0-907590-24-1

Publishing History: This work was first issued in 1931. Some
copies were produced to a standard size, some were printed on
larger paper and had a frontispiece portrait of Neil Munro. This
new edition reproduces the text complete and unabridged with
the addition of a portrait of Neil Munro which is taken from the
edition of *The Bailie* published 24th July 1907.

Published by SPA BOOKS LTD
PO Box 47
STEVENAGE
Herts SG2 8UH

Printed in Great Britain at The Bath Press, Avon

Contents

BOOK I

The Heather

IF I were King of France, that noble fine
    land,
And my gold was elbow-deep in the iron
    chests ;
Were my castles grey and scowling o'er the
    wine-land,
With towers as high as where the eagle nests ;
If harpers sweet, and swordsmen stout and
    vaunting,
My history sang, my stainless tartan wore,
Was not my fortune poor with one thing
    wanting,
    The heather at my door ?

My galleys might be sailing every ocean,
Robbing the isles and sacking hold and keep,
My chevaliers go prancing at my notion,
To bring me back of cattle, horse and sheep ;
Fond arms be round my neck, the young
    heart's tether,
And true love-kisses all the night might fill,
But oh ! *mochree*, if I had not the heather,
    Before me on the hill !

A hunter's fare is all I would be craving,
A shepherd's plaiding and a beggar's pay,
If I might earn them where the heather,
    waving,
Gave grandeur to the day.
The stars might see me, homeless one and
    weary,
Without a roof to fend me from the dew,
And still content, I'd find a bedding cheery
    Where'er the heather grew !

Home

HERE is the shore, and the far wide world's
    before me,
    And the sea says " Come ! " but I would not
    part from you ;
Of gold nor fame would I take for the scent
    of birches
    That hangs around you in the rain or
    dew.
Place of my people, place of the old brave
    stories,
Good hearts, stout hearts, keen swords, and
    their manly glories !

Some will be singing their love for beauteous
    maidens,
    The neck that is white like milk, and the
    sloe-dark eye ;
Maids age and alter, my grief !, but love—my
    own place,
    You show no difference as the years go by.
If I were a roamer returning across the sea
After long years, you would still have the smile
    for me.

I have my friends on the heathy and myrtled
    hill-side,
  In the crowded glens, too, or skiffs so swift
    and bold,
Chasing the red deer far, or mounting the long
    wave,
  Or, the sweet ones !, singing at dusk in the
    turfy fold ;
They have not gear nor land, maybe, nor the
    scholar's lore,
But sure there's the welcome for me at the
    poorest door !

I might be namely, they say, and I might have
    fortune
  Could I but leave you awhile and go away,
But what was my gaining, a wanderer far from
    Aora,
  Where the fish in the brown linns plout,
    where the wild ducks play ?
If the night crept deep and warm, and I astray,
Would my heart not ache for the bird-pipe on
    the spray ?

'Tis ill to say it, for it's only a boyish softness,
  But standing at morning alone on Dunchuach
    high,
To see all my dear place spread wide around
    and below me,

18

Brings the tear that stings to the loving and
greedy eye.
The glen and the corrie, the ben and the sounding shore
Have something that searches me in to the
deepest core !

Oh ! here's a cup to my friends and my
darling own place !
Glad am I that by fortune my mother she
bore me here.
It might have been far on the plains of the
Saxon stranger,
With never a hill like Dunchuach or Dun-
torvil near,
And never a fir with its tassels to toss in the
wind,
Salt Fyne of the fish before, and Creag Dubh
of the deer behind !

Duror of Appin

BLYTHE were the seasons when we were in
    Duror together,
In Appin of stories, and songs of brave old
    tribulations ;
Shores of the sheldrake, hills of the deer, and
    the nut-woods,
        Our hearts like a bird in the bosom !

Gay was it then with us, all the young jovial
    fellows—
Many a dance with the girls in Macgillivray's
    kitchen !
Many a creel-full of peats did we burn till the
    morning
        Shone through the flowers in the
        window.

Green, green the land of Ardgour, oh,
    splendid with thunders !
How from the sheltering milk-house we
    watched its lightnings

Splinter on Garven and rip the veils of the
valley,
    Hearkening the roar of its torrents !

Winds might be scourging then, slashing with
sleet of December ;
Little they vexed us, keeping our trysts with
the maidens,
Whistling our way through the Christmas
glens in the gloaming,
    For the touch of warm lips, and a whisper.

Ah, we were dauntless in those days, the morn
on our bucklers,
Naught was amiss with the world then, we
under enchantments.
Better a day at the trout in the burn or the
moor-cock in Appin,
    Than years of this trade as a soldier !

Had I my wish this day, I would be sailing
Loch Lhinne,
Staving my way on a skiff to the house of
Kingairloch,
Seeking the lad that I was in the years that
were jaunty,
    And She at the tiller beside me !

If they bury me here in the body, my cairn
    among strangers,
Only my bones will abide, for the best of me's
    yonder,
Forever at prime of the morn, age nor care on
    my shoulder.
    In Duror, my Duror of Appin !

IV

Nettles

O SAD for me Glen Aora,
   Where I have friends no more,
For lowly lie the rafters,
   And the lintels of the door.
The friends are all departed,
   The hearth-stone's black and cold,
And sturdy grows the nettle
   On the place beloved of old.

O! black might be that ruin
   Where my fathers dwelt so long,
And nothing hide the shame of it,
   The ugliness and wrong ;
The cabar and the corner-stone
   Might bleach in wind and rains,
But for the gentle nettle
   That took such a courtier's pains.

Here's one who has no quarrel
   With the nettle thick and tall,
That hides the cheerless hearthstone
   And screens the humble wall,

That clusters on the footpath
　Where the children used to play,
And guards a household's sepulchre
　From all who come the way.

There's deer upon the mountain,
　There's sheep along the glen,
The forests hum with feather,
　But where are now the men ?
Here's but my mother's garden
　Where soft the footsteps fall,
My folk are quite forgotten,
　But the nettle's over all.

Monaltree

(*Isle Tiree*)

THE mornings came like sweethearts there,
  And whistled me from bed,
      Monaltree! Monaltree!
Never a care had I, but up
And followed where they led.
Brave little streams were flowing there,
Tansy and thyme were growing there,
Scenting the bland winds blowing there
That once could blow the breath of life
  In me if I were dead.
      Monaltree! Monaltree!

Gay was the world was in it then,
  Nothing at all to rue,
      Monaltree! Monaltree!
A bird was in the breast o' me,
  My step was light's the dew.
I mind the sea-gull's crying then,
Myself I could be flying then!
There was no dule nor dying then,
Going to bed and sleep again
  The only grief I knew,
      Monaltree! Monaltree!

At night when I'm remembering,
  My loss must vex me still,
    Monaltree! Monaltree!
The gallant days all over with,
  Joy gone from wave and hill.
No more for me the breeze is there,
Nor He among the trees is there,
But sorrow of the seas is there;
No more the sweetheart morns will come
  And whistle me where I will,
    Monaltree! Monaltree!

To Exiles

ARE you not weary in your distant places,
  Far, far from Scotland of the mist and
    storm,
In drowsy airs, the sun-smite on your faces,
  The days so long and warm ?
When all around you lie the strange fields
    sleeping,
  The dreary woods where no fond memories
    roam,
Do not your sad hearts over seas come leaping
  To the highlands and the lowlands of your
    Home ?

Wild cries the Winter, loud through all our
    valleys ;
  The midnights roar, the grey noons echo
    back ;
Round steep storm-bitten coasts the eager
    galleys
  Beat for kind harbours from horizons black ;
We tread the miry roads, the rain-drenched
    heather,
  We are the men, we battle, we endure !

God's pity for you people in your weather
  Of swooning winds, calm seas, and skies
    demure !

Wild cries the Winter, and we walk song-
    haunted
  Over the moors and by the thundering falls,
Or where the dirge of a brave past is chaunted
  In dolorous dusks by immemorial walls.
Though rains may thrash on us, the great mists
    blind us,
  And lightning rend the pine-tree on the hill,
Yet are we strong, yet shall the morning find
    us
  Children of tempest all unshaken still.

We wander where the little grey towns cluster
  Deep in the hills, or selvedging the sea,
By farm-lands lone, by woods where wildfowl
    muster
  To shelter from the day's inclemency ;
And night will come, and then far through the
    darkling,
  A light will shine out in the sounding glen,
And it will mind us of some fond eye's spark-
    ling,
  And we'll be happy then.

Let torrents pour then, let the great winds rally,
 Snow-silence fall or lightning blast the pine ;
That light of Home shines warmly in the valley,
 And, exiled son of Scotland, it is thine.
Far have you wandered over seas of longing,
 And now you drowse, and now you well
  may weep,
When all the recollections come a-thronging
 Of this rude country where your fathers
  sleep.

They sleep, but still the hearth is warmly
  glowing,
 While the wild Winter blusters round their
  land ;
That light of Home, the wind so bitter blowing—
 Do they not haunt your dreams on alien
  strand ?
Love, strength, and tempest—oh, come back
  and share them !
 Here's the old cottage, here the open door ;
Fond are our hearts although we do not bare
  them,—
 They're yours, and you are ours for evermore.

BOOK II

BOOK II

I

Processional

I MUST be rising and I must be going
On the roads of magic that stretch afar,
By the random rivers so finely flowing
And under the restless star.
I must be roving on the roads of glory,
So I'll up and shoe me with red-deer hide.
For youth must be learning the ancient story—
Let the wearied oldsters bide.

II

John o' Lorn

My plaid is on my shoulder and my boat is on
the shore,
And it's all bye wi' auld days and you ;
Here's a health and here's a heartbreak, for it's
hame, my dear, no more,
To the green glens, the fine glens we knew !

'Twas for the sake o' glory, but oh ! wae upon
the wars,
That brought my father's son to sic a day ;
I'd rather be a craven, wi' nor name, nor fame,
nor scars,
Than turn a wanderer's heel on Moidart Bay.

And you, in the day-time, you'll be here, and
in the mirk,
Wi' the kind heart, the open hand, and
free ;
And far awa' in foreign France, in town or
camp or kirk,
I'll be wondering if you keep a thought for
me.

But nevermore the heather nor the bracken at
     my knees,
  I'm poor John o' Lorn, a broken man ;
For an auld Hielan' story I must sail the swing-
     ing seas,
  A chief without a castle or a clan.

My plaid is on my shoulder and my boat is on
     the shore,
  And it's all bye wi' auld days and you ;
Here's a health and here's a heartbreak, for it's
     hame, my dear, no more,
  To the green glens, the fine glens we knew !

III

The Kilt's my Delight

WOOL from the mountain, dyes from the vale,
  Loom in the clachan, peat-fires bright ;
To every strand of it some old tale—
  Oh the tartan kilt is my delight !
Went to its spinning brave songs of Lorn ;
  Its hues from the berry and herb were spilt ;
Lilts of the forest and glee of morn
  Are in his walking who wears the kilt !

For priest nor clerk nor merchant men,
  Nor biders at home was the pleating pressed,
But for the loins of those who ken
  Hill-wandering, offspring of the mist ;
Wood-trackers, waders of wild streams,
  The world their pillow, their roof the night ;
Who sleeps in tartan has high dreams,
  Oh the kilt of the Highlands is my delight !

I will put on me that gallant gear,
  Brave first garb of the human kind,
Travel the moors and the hills of deer,
  And feel on my body the kiss of the wind.

Be it melting heat or the driven sleet,
　　Kings to stand with or foes to fight,
Dance in the shealing, or death to meet,
　　Oh the darling kilt is my delight !

Bannocks o' Barley

JUST gie us a griddle, a guid Cu'-ross griddle,
　　A neivefu' o' salt and the side o' a burn,
We'll feed like our fathers that never kent
　　　famine,
　　Wi' meal and a griddle nae Scottie'll mourn!
It's no' the day's provand that makes ye the
　　　sodger,
　　It's milk o' your mother that fills ye wi' steel;
And sae we'll be couthy, and sae we'll be canty,
　　As lang's we hae bannocks o' barley meal.

The Englishman's kyte is a great tribulation,
　　He must hae kitchen, and puddins, and wine;
A pokefu' o' meal frae the Lothians for Donald,
　　A faggot o' wood and a well, and he'll dine!
Gie us the meal and we'll soon find the collops,
　　But if they're no' in it, ye'll no' hear us
　　　squeal;
Our fathers before us were dour folk to meddle,
　　Wi' naething but bannocks o' barley meal.

For dance or for battle it's best to be meagre,
　　Keep down the waist o' ye, lank be your
　　　frame;

Endurance and elegance, youth, love and
  daring
  Depend on the belt ye can put round your
  wame.
Praise God we were born where our food was
  to fight for,
  The land o' the barley's the land o' the leal;
It gave us but love and a song and a story,
  And bred us on bannocks o' barley meal.

Take to the hills on the wings o' the mornin',
  Bed on the heather and breath o' the gale;
Be stark as the Coolins and lean as the larch-
  tree,
  And 'gainst ye nae powers in Hell will
  prevail.
It's only yestreen we were poor as a piper,
  We've lived near the bone and we've
  flourished on't weel,
At the worst it's just back to auld brose and
  brochan,
  Our lassies'll bake us the barley meal!
      Bannocks o' barley! bannocks o'
        barley!
      Bannocks o' barley meal!

V

Sergeant o' Pikes

WHEN I sat in the service o' foreign com-
   manders,
   Selling my sword for a beggar-man's fee,
Learning the trade o' the warrior who
   wanders,
   To mak' ilka stranger a sworn enemie ;
There was ae thought that nerved me, and
   brawly it served me
   With pith to the claymore wherever I
   won,
'Twas the auld sodger's story, that, gallows or
   glory,
   The Hielan's, the Hielan's were crying me
   on !

I tossed upon swinging seas, splashed to my
   kilted knees,
   Ocean or ditch it was ever the same ;
In leaguer or sally, tattoo or revally,
   The message on every pibroch that came,
Was " Cruachan, Cruachan, O son remember
   us,
   Think o' your fathers and never be
   slack ! "

Blade and buckler together, though far off the
heather,
The Hielan's, the Hielan's were all at my
back !

The ram to the gate-way, the torch to the
tower,—
We rifled the kist, and the cattle we maimed ;
Our dirks stabbed at guess through the leaves
o' the bower,
And crimes we committed that needna be
named :
Moonlight or dawning grey, Lammas or Lady-
day,
Donald maun dabble his plaid in the
gore ;
He maun hough and maun harry, or should he
miscarry,
The Hielan's, the Hielan's will own him no
more !

A Sergeant o' Pikes, I have pushed and have
parried O,
My heart still at tether in bonny Glenshee ;
Weary the marches made, sad the towns
harried O,
But the bonny green heather was aye at my
knee :—

The hill-berry mellowing, stag-o'-ten bellow-
        ing,
The song o' the fold and the tale by the
        hearth,
Bairns at the crying and auld wives a-dying—
The Hielan's sent wi' me to fight round the
        earth !

VI

Come to us, and we will give you Flesh

(*Clanranald Pibroch*)

THERE'S flesh in the glen for ye, raven and
  eagle,
  There's fire in the thatch, and there's death
  in the corn ;
We fed on hot fury, for you the cold leav-
  ings,
  Why starve ye in Moidart when plenty's in
  Lorn ?
Come from your mountains and sup in Glen-
  orchy,
  Where's left but the sound of the wind and
  the burn—
There's nothing to scare ye, dark birds of
  Clanranald—
  The Campbells are gone and they'll never
  return !

God's name ! they provoked us, the crook-
  mouthed, the cunning !
  Sitting so pious and snug in their holds,

Their eyes shut in prayer till the fat rings
   rolled o'er them,
   A blame and a boast in each bleat from their
   folds.
'Twas not that they spoiled us by sword or by
   sheepskin,
   Not that they harried or lifted our kine,—
They passed us at market like dirt from the
   lowlands,
   O children of Diarmaid ! O litter of swine !

The foumart and fox they will suffer no
   taming,
   The twist in the pine-tree can never be
   healed ;
For vermin the gun, then, for crook-wood the
   hatchet,
   Search ye, my gallant birds, where they're
   concealed.
Look in the corn where they're lying like
   divots ;—
   We were of old when the sea-wave was
   fresh ;—
Cruachan will crumble but never Clanranald,
   Grey birds of Moidart, oh come and get
   flesh !

VII

The Fiddle

WHEN I was young, I had no sense,
I bought a fiddle for eighteenpence,
And the only tune that I could play,
Was Over The Hills and Far Away.

To learn another I had no care,
For oh ! it was a bonny air,
And all the wee things of the glen
Came out and gathered round me then.

The furry folk that dwell in wood,
Quitted their hushed green solitude,
Came round about me, unafraid,
And skipped to the music that I made.

Birds of the moor, birds of the tree
Took up the tune with fiddle and me ;
Happy were we on that summer day
With Over The Hills and Far Away.

I hied me up on the lone hill road
Where the Little Green People have their
abode,
And fiddled to them on the ruined cairn
Till they all came out from the rush and fern.

With gossamer threads the fields were laid,
  That shimmered like silk where the sunlight
    played,
Quick over them hurried the fairy throng
  And danced to the strains of the darling song.

Their gowns were made of the linnet's feather,
  Their hats of the purple bells of heather,
And oh! how they chuckled with elfin glee
  To the zig-a-zig-zig of my minstrelsy!

'Twas I was the Captain of that band
  That played with me in fairy land,
Till the moon leaned over the hills to stare,
  And see who fiddled the fairy air.

Fr-r-rip!—the furry folk turned and fled,
  And every bird to the thicket sped.
In a flash my fairy friends were gone,
  And fiddle and I were all alone.

I sold my fiddle to buy a drum,
  But never again did the fairies come,
And all the bliss of that happy day
  Is Over the Hills and Far Away.

VIII

Hail to thee, and Fare-thee-well!

HAIL to thee, and fare-thee-well!
　　Unstable, cold as sleet,
Broken is the childish spell
　　That held me at your feet.

I know now how the land beguiles,
　　How cunning is the sea;
It was the magic of the isles
　　Alone enchanted me.

The birken trees, with sly intent,
　　Waved round your walk their grace,
Majestic mountains o'er you lean't,
　　Transfiguring your face;

Perfumes that from the moor arise,
　　I thought came from your hair,
It was the sea looked in your eyes,
　　And mirrored blueness there.

That voice so sweet on heathy bens
　　Which now my heart recalls—

Naught but the glamour of the glens
  Sounding with water-falls !

Maternal nature's petted child,
  Tricked out to dupe and please,
All false with fascination wild,
  Lent by the Hebrides !

Those evening raptures I confessed,
  Contemplating your mind,
Were but the influence of the mist,
  The star-shine and the wind.

Farewell ! the bagpipe's battle air
  Completes my wakening ;
It calls me from these isles to where
  A truer love is beckoning.

There is no witchery for me
  In the far land of the stranger,
And steadfastness must ever be
  In the bold true eyes of danger !

BOOK III

I

Lament for Macleod of Raasay

ALLAN IAN ÒG MACLEOD of Raasay,
  Treasure of mine, lies yonder dead in Loos,
His body unadorned by Highland raiment,
  Trammelled, for glorious hours, in Saxon
    trews.
Never man before of all his kindred
  Went so apparelled to the burial knowe,
But with the pleated tartan for his shrouding,
  The bonnet on his brow.

My grief! that Allan should depart so sadly,
  When no wild mountain pipe his bosom
    wrung,
With no one of his race beside his shoulder
  Who knew his history and spoke his
    tongue!
Ah! lonely death and drear for darling
  Allan!
  Before his ghost had taken wings and gone,
Loud would he cry in Gaelic to his gallants,
  " Children of storm, press on ! "

Beside him, when he fell there in his beauty,
　　Macleods of all the islands should have died ;
Brave hearts his English !—but they could not
　　　　fathom
　　　To what old deeps the voice of Allan cried ;
When in that strange French country-side war-
　　　　battered,
　　　Far from the creeks of home and hills of
　　　　heath,
A boy, he kept the old tryst of his people
　　With the dark girl Death.

Oh Allan Ian Òg !   Oh Allan aluinn !
　　Sore is my heart remembering the past,
And you of Raasay's ancient gentle children
　　The farthest-wandered, kindliest and last !
It should have been the brave dead of the
　　　islands
　　　That heard ring o'er their tombs your battle
　　　cry,
To shake them from their sleep again, and
　　　quicken
　　　Peaks of Torridon and Skye.

Gone in the mist the brave Macleods of Raasay,
　　Far furth from fortune, sundered from their
　　　lands,
And now the last grey stone of Castle Raasay,
　　Lies desolate and levelled with the sands.

But pluck the old isle from its roots deep-
   planted
  Where tides cry coronach round the
   Hebrides,
And it will bleed of the Macleods lamented,
  Their loves and memories !

II

Pipes in Arras

In the borough toun of Arras
  When gloaming had come on,
Fifty pipers played Retreat
  As if they had been one,
And the Grande Place of Arras
  Hummed with the Highland drone.

Then to that ravaged borough,
  Champed into dust and sand,
Came with the pipers' playing,
  Out of their own loved land,
Sea-sounds that moan for sorrow
  On a dispeopled strand.

There are in France no voices
  To speak of simple things,
And tell how winds will whistle
  Through palaces of kings ;
Now came the truth to Arras
  In the chanter's warblings.

" O build in pride your towers,
  But think not they will last ;
The tall tower and the shealing
  Alike must meet the blast,

And the world is strewn with shingle
From dwellings of the past."

But to the Grande Place, Arras,
    Came, too, the hum of bees,
That suck the sea-pink's sweetness
    From isles of the Hebrides,
And in Iona fashion
    Homes 'mid old effigies.

" Our cells the monks demolished
    To make their mead of yore,
And still though we be ravished
    Each Autumn of our store,
While the sun lasts and the flowers,
    Tireless we'll gather more."

Up then and spake with twitt'rings,
    Out of the chanter reed,
Birds that each Spring to Appin,
    Over the oceans speed,
And in its ruined castles,
    Make love again and breed.

" Already see our brothèrs
    Build in the tottering fane !
Though France should be a desert,
    While love and Spring remain
Men will come back to Arras,
    And build and weave again."

So played the pipes in Arras
    Their Gaelic symphony,
Filled with old wisdom gathered
    In isles of the Highland sea,
And eastward towards Cambrai
    Roared the artillery.

III

Fingal's Weeping

BECAUSE they were so brave and young
    Who now are sleeping,
His old heart wrung, his harp unstrung,
    Fingal's a-weeping.
There's warble of waters at morning in Etive
    glen,
    And the birds loud-crying;
Chuckle of Spring in the wood, on the moor,
    on the ben;
    No heed for their dying!
So Fingal's weeping the young brave
    sleeping;
    Fingal's weeping.

They'll be forgot—in Time—forgot!
    Time that goes sweeping;
The wars they fought remembered not,
    And Fingal's weeping.
Hearken for voices of sorrow for them in the
    forest den
    Where once they were rovers—
Only the birds of the wild at their building again;
    Whispering of lovers!
So Fingal's weeping, his old grief keeping,
    Fingal's weeping.

They should be mourned by the ocean
    wave
  Round lone isles creeping,
But the laughing wave laments no grave,
  And Fingal's weeping.
Morvern and Moidart, glad, gallant and gay
    in the sun,
  Rue naught departed,
The moon and the stars shine out when day is
    done,
  Cold, stony-hearted.
So Fingal's weeping war's red reaping,
  Fingal's weeping !

IV

Hey, Jock, are ye glad ye 'listed?

Hey! Jock, are ye glad ye 'listed?
  O Jock, but ye're far frae hame!
What d'ye think o' the fields o' Flanders?
  Jockey lad, are ye glad ye came?
Wet rigs we wrought in the land o' Lennox,
  When Hielan' hills were smeared wi' snaw;
Deer we chased through the seepin' heather,
  But the glaur o' Flanders dings them a'!

This is no' Fair o' Balloch,
  Sunday claes and a penny reel;
It's no' for dancin' at a bridal
  Willie Lawrie's bagpipes squeal.
Men are to kill in the morn's mornin';
  Here we're back to your daddy's trade;
Naething for't but to cock the bonnet,
  Buckle on graith and kiss the maid.

The Cornal's yonder deid in tartan,
  Sinclair's sheuched in Neuve Eglise;
Slipped awa wi' the sodger's fever,
  Kinder than ony auld man's disease.

Scotland ! Scotland ! little we're due ye,
 Poor employ and skim-milk board.
But youth's a cream that maun be paid for,
 We got it reamin', so here's the sword !

Come awa, Jock, and cock your bonnet,
 Swing your kilt as best ye can ;
Auld Dumbarton's Drums are dirlin',
 Come awa, Jock, and kill your man !
Far's the cry to Leven Water
 Where your fore-folks went to war,
They would swap wi' us to-morrow,
 Even in the Flanders glaur !

V

The Only Son

YOUNG Alasdair of Oolava is dead
In the dark and over the deep,
The world for his pillow, the wind his plaid,
And I live on and weep !
From the hour when they put him on my
    knee,
I knew, my grief, what the end would be ;
I knew before he gave smile or sigh,
It was not at home his bones would lie,
That he would love and travel and die,
And leave me alone in Oolava.

At night I am crying along the shore :
" O Alasdair, here is home ! "
And leave for your welcome the open door,—
Not even your ghost will come !
It must walk sad sands in the foreign lands,
In blindness and blackness with outstretched
    hands,
Too far, too far over sundering seas,
Too far from your folk in the Hebrides
For our poor dirging to give you ease,
Oolava ! Oolava ! Oolava !

Did I know this night where my dead son
Walks bloody with his chief,
Would I not put plaid on my head and run
Through the last black gate of grief,
To walk by his side and bring to his mind
The darling isle and the folk so kind?
For it's dark in Death where you are lost,
My Alasdair, my wandering ghost;
And far is the cry from that cursed coast
To the little isle of Oolava!

VI

Romance

OLD orchard crofts of Picardy,
  In the high warm winds of May,
Hummed in a froth of blossom,
  And spattered the roads with spray.
Over the earth the scudding cloud,
  And the laverock whistling high,
Lifted the drooping heart of the lad
  At one bound to the sky ;
France ! France ! and the old romance
  Came over him like a spell,
Home-sickness and his weariness
  Shook from him then and fell,
    For he was again with D'Artagnan,
    With Alan Breck and D'Artagnan ;
    And the pipes that went before him
    Were playing airs of Pan.

Through dust that in a mist uprose
  From under the tramping feet,
He saw the storied places dim
  In the haze of the summer heat.
Menace and ambush, wounds and death,
  Lurked in the ditch and wood,

But he, high-breasted, walked in joy
 With a glorious multitude.
Great hearts that never perish,
 Nor grow old with the aches of Time,
Marched through the morning with him,
 All in a magic clime.
  But loved of all were D'Artagnan,
  And Alan the kith of kings,
  Fond comrades of his childhood,
  Still on their wanderings.

From miry clefts of the wintry plain
 He leapt with his platoon,
The morion on his forehead
 And the sould of him at noon.
With head high to the hurricane
 He walked, and in his breast
He knew himself immortal,
 And that death was but a jest.
A smile was on his visage
 When they found him where he fell,
The gallant old companions,
 Dreaming on asphodel.
  " Lad o' my heart ! " cried Alan Breck,
  " Well done thy first campaign ! "
  "Sleep thou till morn," said D'Artagnan,
  " When we three march again."

VII

The Brattie

THE brattie for sweepin', the brattie for
   dirt!
Tie on your brattie and tuck up your shirt!
It's always the case when there's cleanin'
   to do
That the first for the besom's the Bonnets o'
   Blue.
Once we were gentry and cleaned in the
   kilt,
Wi' a braw Hielan' sporran and money
   'ntil't;
Now deil to the sporran! and tartan's *napoo*;
It's ower guid for the work and it's put out o'
   view
Below the brown brattie for sweepin'!

The mothers that bore us—the best ever
   stept!—
Were up in the mornin' when other folk
   slept;
Do ye think they were deckin' themsel's in the
   glass,
Or plannin' diversions to mak' the day
   pass?

E

Na, na! the wee mothers, the dainty and
  dour,
Were up at revally to fight wi' the stour—
That the hame might be tidy, and children be
  spruce,
They swept like the winds o' the hill through
  the hoose,
And bonny they looked in their bratties!

Dirt will come down on ye, dae what ye
  can,
And cleanin' a steadin's a task for a man,
So we're up like our mothers at screigh o' the
  dawn,
Sarks up to the elbows and aprons on.
The thing to mak' Europe as clean as a
  whistle
'S a besom o' heath frae the land o' the thistle,
A besom o' heath and a wash o' the sea;
The breeks for our sailors, for us the bare
  knee,
And the brattie, the brattie o' Scotland!

If ever we fight wi' true gentry again,
We'll go in full tartan and meet them like
  men.
Our sporrans 'll glitter, our feathers 'll wave,
To honour a foe that is gallant and brave;

But for mucking a midden and cleanin' out
    swine
That's needin' a duckin' in water o' Rhine,
It were silly to dress in our Sunday array,
So we'll dress like our work as our mothers
    would say,
And that's wi' the bonny brown brattie !

VIII

Wild Rover Lads

UNCOVENANTED godless race,
Astray and under spells,
We left for you the promised grace,
    And sought nane for oursels.

Our souls might be in jeopardy,
As lang's our blood ran hot,
But surely we're assoiled and free
    Now that we've paid our shot.

Mickle we missed, be it confessed,
That brings auld age content ;
Blaw the wind East, or blaw it West,
    'Twas there wi' a sang we went.

Moon in the glen, youth in the blood,
Sent us stravaigin' far,
Ower late ! ower late in the whisperin' wood,
    So we saw nae mornin' star.

Deep, deep we drank in tavern lands,
For the sake o' companie,
And some o' us wrecked on Young Man
    Sands,
    Ere ever we got to sea.

We had nae need for the parish bell,
But still—when the bugle cried,
We went for you to Neuve Chapelle,
We went for you to the yetts o' hell,
And there for you we died !

IX

Lochaber no More

FAREWELL to Lochaber, farewell to the glen,
  No more will he wander Lochaber again.
Lochaber no more!   Lochaber no more!
  The lad will return to Lochaber no more!
The trout will come back from the deeps of the
    sea,
  The bird from the wilderness back to the
    tree,
Flowers to the mountain, and tides to the shore,
  But he will return to Lochaber no more!

Oh why should the hills last, that never were
    young,
  Unperishing stars in the heavens be hung;
Be constant the seasons, undrying the stream,
  And he that was gallant be gone like a
    dream?
Brave songs will be singing in lands of the West,
  But he will be silent who sang them the
    best;
The dance will be waiting, the pipes will
    implore,
  But he will return to Lochaber no more!

Child of the forest ! profound is your sleep ;
  Lochaber that loved you awakes but to
    weep ;
When our fires are rekindled at dawn of the
    morn,
  Our griefs burn afresh, and our prayers are
    forlorn ;
The night falls disconsolate, bringing no peace,
  No hope for our dreams, for our sighs no
    release ;
In vain when the Spring comes we look from
    the door,
  For he will return to Lochaber no more !

X

The Bells o' Banff

As I gaed down the water side,
  I heard a maiden sing,
All in the lee-lone Sabbath morn,
  And the green glen answering,—
" No longer hosts encountering hosts,
  Shall clouds of slain deplore,
They hang the trumpet in the hall,
  And study war no more."

Dead men of ancient tumults lay
  In dust below her feet,
Their spirits breathed to her but scents
  Of mint and the meadow-sweet.
Singing her psalm, her bosom calm
  As the dappled sky above,
She thought the world was dedicate
  For evermore to love !

O God ! my heart was like to break,
  Hearing her guileless strain,
For pipes screamed through the Highland
    hills,
  And swords were forth again.

And little did the lassie ken
 Banff's battle-bells were ringing ;
Her lad was in the gear o' war,
 While she was happy singing !

BOOK IV

I

The Story Teller

(R. *L. S.   Dec.* 3, 1894)

BEFORE the firelight in the Winter gloaming,
    The one far-wandered soberly will tell
The brave memorials of his weary roaming,
    And like a warlock hold us in his spell,
Till, sudden, at the lozen comes a rapping—
    " O Sennachie, I'd speak wi' ye my son ! "
The wanderer for the cold night must be
       happing
    The cup unfinished and the tale half-done.

And when the door is snecked behind the
       rover
    Who went wi' yon Convoy we need not
       name,
We tell again his gallant stories over,
    The thought in every heart of us the same—
" O fine were these the tales that he narrated,
    But there were others that he had in
       store ;
Ours was the gain had he a little waited,
    But now our ears are vain for evermore ! "

So you are happed and gone, and there you're
      lying,
    Far from the glens, deep down the slope of
      seas,
Out of the stormy night, the grey sleet flying,
    And never again for you the Hebrides !
We need not keep the peat and cruisie glowing,
    The goodwife may put by her ale and bread,
For you, who kept the crack so blithely going,
    Now sleep at last, silent and comforted.

Our Winter's here, and mists through the glens
      are trailing,
    The constant rain-smirr rots the fallen leaf,
Lost in the years old Ossian's ghosts are
      wailing,
    We'll bar the door and be alone with Grief ;
But one last sprig of Highland heather's
      growing
    Upon the hills of Home that well you knew,
And it (Oh tell him, wind that's southward
      blowing !),
    My Wanderer, my Sennachie's for you !

II

Wild Geese

It was not any songster of the forest
    That brought to me, yon night, unholy fears,
Thrush of the thicket nor the questioning owlet,
    Though these knew all my deeds in those
        wild years ;
It was the grey lag goose that comes to Barra,
    That found me desolate and dry of tears.

I was alone within my winter dwelling,
    My children gone, my peat-fire dead and grey,
Old and unable—I who once was tempest !
    Shivering to hear the rattle of the spray,
When high above my chimney came the wild
        geese,
    And brought my ghosts about me where I
        lay.

Ah ! well I knew they came from gran'ries
        opened,
    Where old mad joys and folly's crops are
        stored,
Grain o' the wild-oat, ready for the grind-stone,
    To make the bitter bread of age abhorred.

My grief! they found me unprepared for
    pardon,
  With all my youth of tumult undeplored !

I had forgot those ancient joys and sinnings,
  And now was far too old for penitence.
From out the north, beyond the seven
    mountains,
    Those grey birds of the evening had brought
    hence
My memories, but no remorse, through dark-
    ness,
  The weeping night, lost fields of innocence.

III

Colin's Cattle

COLIN's cattle have gone astray,
  Far-wandered, under spells ;
To the myrtle of the moorland,
  Thicket, or golden strand.
He has sought them in the oat-fields,
  And by the cressy wells,
And cried for them with weeping
  Along the island sand.
But only the lapwing answers
  To the herd-boy's pleading calls,
Ripple of wind in the rushes,
  The drone of a passing bee ;
Oh love ! my little Colin,
  The autumn evening falls,
Thy cattle are lost to thee !

He has sought them on the sweet grass
  About the kingly tombs—
Nought there but the beetle,
  And the chirrup of the wren !
Stood, fearful, in the birchwood
  Where half-light dwells and glooms,
And heard but fairy chucklings
  Where the badger has his den.

F

Oh grief! for little Colin,
    That he should go asleep
By the wild-bees' store of honey
    In the sound of water-falls;
While the kine were on the sea-wrack
    And their old herds in the deep
To whistle them to fairy stalls!

Ochanie! for Colin's cattle,
    With their rich and salty milk;
Fondly his mother sang to them
    Sea-reiver songs of old;
Coaxed them to their milking
    With a hand as soft as silk,
Strewed the seaweed and the shingle
    In the summer shealing's fold.
"Not common kine are these," she said,
    "Of the beggar landward breed,
But cattle of the Quiet Folk
    That dwell in dun and deep.
Be wakeful little hero, mother's treasure,
    When the tides cry where they feed;
They pass if once you sleep!"

Gone are the eerie cattle
    That browsed sea-weedy bays,
With ever the trout and the herring-scales
    Like gems on their glistening hides;

And the wee white calf of Colin's heart,
    That on winter's stormy days
Ran bleating down to the spindrift,
    And stood knee-deep in tides.
He may call them on the hillock,
    He may search along the shore ;
Weep his way through gloaming
    Till the far sea-lamps are lit ;
They have gone to other pastures,
    He will bring them home no more
To the byre where the blind bats flit.

They have gone, the fairy cattle,
    Across the thyme and thrift,
To where the old sea-meadow life
    With all its joy beguiles ;
To-night they go to milking
    Where the lobsters stare and drift
Around the cavern cow-sheds
    Of the green, salt, swinging kyles.
To-morrow for the skerries
    Where the sea-girls comb their hair,
The sappy sea-plain grazings
    Where the tide rips through the Sound,
But my grief ! my grief ! for Colin
    And the wee calf of his care ;
It will never more be found !

IV

The Tocherless Lass

DRUMORE has a leash of daughters,
  And wants men for the three ;
Six milch-cows go with Juliet,
  And a mare of pedigree ;
With Bell a score of wethers,
  And a share in the fishing-smack,
And nothing at all with Anna
  But the shift upon her back.

Like a deer on the hill is Juliet,
  High breast and proud command,
There's not a tree that's more composed
  Stands on her father's land :
A lad might well surrender
  To that quick and tempting eye—
With six milch-cows at pasture,
  And a fine strong mare forbye.

There is not in all broad Albyn,
  No, nor in the realm of France,
The like of Bell the dainty one
  When she steps out to dance :

She sings to beat the thrush at morn,
   Over her milking-dish,
And she has the black-faced wethers
   And an eighth part of the fish.

But there's something about Anna
   Like a gay, brave day in June;
Though I canna put the words to't
   I could whistle't to a tune;
The king himself would cock his hat,
   And stop for to admire,
Even if she were a gipsy lass
   By a roadside fire.

Ah! cunning man is Cameron of Drumore,
   I know him well!
It's the best bird of the clecking
   He would keep last for himsel':
Two-thirds of Patrick's family
   I would not have in gift;
When he brings them to the market,
   I'll have Anna in her shift!

V

Di-Chuimhne

(From the Gaelic)

I HEARD in the glen, when the snowdrifts were
　　heaping,
　　The wailing of women, lamenting of men ;
They kept the graves green with the warmth
　　of their weeping,
　　For lads who would love, laugh, nor battle
　　again.

I stood in the glen, when the woodlands were
　　pealing
　　With airs of the Spring, and the old life went
　　on ;
There was dance on the meadow, and song in
　　the shealing,
　　The graves were still there, but the mourners
　　were gone !

VI

In Prison

(From the French of Paul Verlaine)

OUTSIDE the window, stanchion-barred,
    A gean-tree's wavin',
Through the blue lift abune the yard
    The sun gangs stavin'.

Saft frae the ancient steeple falls
    The toon-bell's ringin',
In good men's gardens ower the walls
    A bird is singin'.

My God! how simple life may be—
    Tranquil, slow-glidin',
There where the folk are douce and free,
    An' law-abidin'.

Oh! you that in the cauld tolbooth
    Greet, broken-hearted,
What hae ye done wi' your braw youth,
    That's now departed?